MW01592437

2014
FIRST LOOK BOOK

NOTES

TBR LIST

PLANNER

FIRST CHAPTER EXCERPTS

HENERY PRESS

2014 FIRST LOOK BOOK
Part of the Henery Press Notes & Quotes Collection

First Edition
Print edition | May 2014

Henery Press
www.henerypress.com

ISBN-13: 978-1-940976-36-5

Printed in the United States of America

"the more that you

READ

THE MORE THINGS YOU WILL KNOW

THE MORE THAT YOU

LEARN

THE MORE PLACES

YOU WILL GO"

- Dr. Seuss,
*I Can Read
with My Eyes Shut!*

DINERS, dives & DEAD ENDS
by Terri L. Austin

Mondays were known for two things at Ma's Diner: we poured lots of extra coffee and the tips sucked. After my last customer left, I counted out my money. Twenty-three dollars and sixteen cents. Hmm, food or gas?

I walked behind the counter and had just started to refill ketchup bottles when my friend, Ax, walked in. The bright afternoon sunshine flashed on his wallet chain as it slapped against his thigh.

66 This cozy mystery was fun! With twists, turns & surprises that left me hanging on right to the end, I couldn't put it down. 99

— *Cozy Mystery Book Reviews*

_____ / _____ / _____

NOTES

_____ / _____ / _____

NOTES

PORTRAIT of a DEAD GUY

by LARISSA REINHART

In a small town, there is a thin gray line between personal freedom and public ruin. Everyone knows your business without even trying. Folks act polite all the while remembering every stupid thing you've done in your life. Not to mention getting tied to all the dumbass stuff your relations—even those dead or gone—have done. We forgive but don't forget.

DAPHNE DU MAURIER
AWARD FINALIST

66 Reinhart is a truly talented author and this book was one of the best cozy mysteries we reviewed this year...
Our Rating: 4.5 Stars. 99

— *Mystery Tribune*

NOTES

Lowcountry BOIL
by *Susan M. Boyer*

The dead are patient.

I know this firsthand. My best friend Colleen drowned in Breach Inlet the spring of our junior year in high school, and I didn't hear a peep out of her until last March–a month after my thirty-first birthday. It was a Friday night, a few minutes past nine, and I had just chased a rabbit into Falls Park, in the West End of Greenville, South Carolina. The rabbit was fast, for one so big. At the foot of the rock steps that led down from the street, he darted under the Liberty Bridge. We'd had a cold snap, and while the sidewalks of downtown Greenville bustled with restaurant traffic, the park was deserted except for me, the rabbit, and my partner, Nate Andrews.

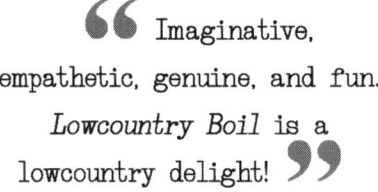

_____ / _____ / _____

NOTES

_____ / _____ / _____

_____ / _____ / _____

NOTES

CROPPED to death

by CHRISTINA FREEBURN

The industrial sized straight-blade trimmer sliced through the air. Even from across the room, I heard the blade going through paper-whoosh, whoosh. I poked a finger into my left ear and pressed the cell against the other. My grandmother Hope's instructions garbled through the device, the words loud and then soft, an effect that had nothing to do with being in a technological dead zone. Not that keeping a cell phone connection was easy to do in Eden, West Virginia.

Since we started the Scrap This employee crop two hours ago, the whacking hadn't stopped. The blade, like my sanity, was near breaking. I covered the mouthpiece and leaned across the front counter, trying to catch Marilyn's gaze as I avoided jamming my side into the cash register. "Could you adhere something for a while?"

66 Witty,
entertaining and fun
with a side of murder. 99

— Shelley Giusti,
Shelley's Book Case

NOTES

LAST diner STANDING
by Terri L. Austin

There are some absolutes in this life that are irrefutable. If you leave the house looking like crap, you'll see someone you know, usually an ex-boyfriend. If you're running late for an appointment, you'll hit every red light on the way. And a three a.m. phone call is never good news. Either someone's dead, in the hospital, or you're a drunken booty call. But that Saturday morning, I discovered another reason to avoid the ringing harbinger of bad news.

66 Austin's second course
has the menu of a
feisty underemployed gal detective
with a side order of romance
down pat. **99**

— *Kirkus Reviews*

NOTES

_____ / _____ / _____

NOTES

OTHER PEOPLE'S BAGGAGE

Three Interconnected Mystery Novellas

MIDNIGHT ICE by Diane Vallere

I started my getaway on the floor. And by floor, I mean the beige speckled linoleum tile squares that covered the ground by the Monterey Airport baggage claim. A fragile-looking Chihuahua broke free from the grasp of a young girl and ran over to sniff me.

SWITCH BACK by Kendel Lynn

The wheels of our flight touched down in Waco, Texas at half-past eleven on a very late hot August night. I would've been so much happier had those wheels touched down at Dallas/Fort Worth since that's where we were heading...

FOOL'S GOLD by Gigi Pandian

I stepped onto the stage of the theater. The spotlight blinded me, but after a few seconds my eyes began to adjust. The stage was nearly empty. To my left, a wooden wardrobe cabinet. To my right, a weathered whisky barrel that had seen better days.

66 Your first class ticket to three fast-paced adventures full of mystery, murder, and magic! 99

— Elizabeth Craig,
Author of the Southern Quilting Series

NOTES

FRONT PAGE FATALITY
by LynDee Walker

Thinking about blood spatters and ballistics reports before I'd even finished my coffee wasn't exactly how I wanted to start my weekend.

"More dead people? Really, guys?" I asked, as if the beat cops whose chatter blared out of the police scanner in my passenger seat could hear me. They, of course, kept right on talking. Apparently, this dead guy had lost a good bit of brains to a bullet, too.

AGATHA AWARD
NOMINEE

66 Delightful,
with engaging characters,
a crackling good mystery,
and of course, high, high heels...
What fun! 99

— Harley Jane Kozak,
Agatha and Anthony Award-Winning Author

NOTES

_____ / _____ / _____

____ / ____ / ____

NOTES

malicious masquerade
by ALAN CUPP

At seven minutes before the scheduled start of his six-thirty wedding, Tyler Moore had yet to be seen by anyone at the church. Billy, the best man, stood outside on the front steps of the massive cathedral and nervously took a long drag on his cigarette.

The light June breeze scattered ashes on his black tux. He brushed them off with his hand while he continuously scanned the street for his buddy's car.

After one last puff, Billy dropped the cigarette to the concrete and ground at it with his shiny black shoes before stepping back inside the church.

NOTES

BOARD STIFF

By Kendel Lynn

I'm embarrassed to admit my most vivid memory of that night is of ten minutes in the library with Nick Ransom. In my defense, three of those minutes were damn good minutes, and I had no idea the murder of a colleague was only a few hours away.

AGATHA AWARD
NOMINEE

66 A solid and satisfying mystery, yes indeed, and the fabulous and funny Elliott Lisbon is a true gem! Engaging, clever and genuinely delightful. **99**

— Hank Phillippi Ryan,
Agatha, and Anthony Award-Winning Author

NOTES

_____ / _____ / _____

NOTES

DOUBLE WHAMMY

by Gretchen Archer

A little unemployment goes a long, long way, and after more than a year of it, applying for every available position in L.A. (Lower Alabama), I took a right and tried Mississippi. At the end of the road I found Biloxi, where instead of applying for fifty different jobs, I applied for the same job, fifty different times.

USA TODAY
BESTSELLER

❝ Archer navigates a satisfyingly complex plot and injects plenty of humor as she goes. This madcap debut is a winning hand for fans of Janet Evanovich and Deborah Coonts. ❞

— *Library Journal*

NOTES

STILL LIFE IN BRUNSWICK STEW
by LARISSA REINHART

They should've kept the mud pit.

That was my first thought when I heard another brawl had ensued, the second or third of the day by my count. This happens when festival committees get all high-brow and replace four-wheeling with an arts and crafts display. What kind of crazy wants to walk around an old cotton field to shop for macramé pot holders and corn husk dolls? Or even quality art, like my Cherry Tucker still life oil paintings. Or exquisite Raku pottery from my buddy, Eloise Parker.

That's my opinion, anyway. Based on the fact that the Annual Sidewinder Brunswick Stew Cook-Off took place smack dab in the middle of a Georgia summer when you needed activities like mud pits to cool off the locals.

66 This mystery keeps you laughing and guessing from the first page to the last. A whole-hearted five stars. 99

— Denise Grover Swank,
New York Times Bestselling Author

NOTES

_____ / _____ / _____

NOTES

ARTIFACT
BY GIGI PANDIAN

The door of the house swung open before I had a chance to knock. It was almost midnight. The woman in front of me was fully dressed and held a cup of coffee in her hand, which I hoped for her sake was decaffeinated. Her face was in shadow as she stood in the door frame of the San Francisco Victorian, but the dim porch light must have illuminated all of me down to my toes, for I heard her breath catch.

"Is that blood on your shoe?" Nadia asked.

USA TODAY
BESTSELLER

SUSPENSE MAGAZINE
BEST OF 2012

66 *Artifact* is witty, clever, and twisty...Do you like Agatha Christie? Elizabeth Peters? Then you're going to love Gigi Pandian. **99**

— Aaron Elkins
Edgar Award-Winning Author

NOTES

THE AMBITIOUS CARD

BY JOHN GASPARD

Ask anyone and they'll tell you I'm generally a positive person. But even I had to admit, this was a bad situation.

After the heavy wooden door closed behind us with an unforgiving finality, I'd come to a sudden insight—when it comes to being in the dark, there's dark-dark and then there's inside-a-cave dark.

We were definitely in the latter.

❝ This is a hugely entertaining crime novel... Warm, funny and well plotted— a book to brighten any grey day. Do read it! **❞**

— *Fiction Fan's Book Reviews*

NOTES

_____ / _____ / _____

___ / ___ / ___

NOTES

Lowcountry BOMBSHELL
by Susan M. Boyer

The dead are not troubled by the passage of time. I know this because my best girlfriend, Colleen, died when we were seventeen. She hasn't aged a day in fourteen years. I turned thirty-one last February and commenced researching wrinkle creams.

My familiarity with the departed accounts for why, on that steamy Wednesday in late July, I entertained the notion that the blonde on my front porch was the ghost of Marilyn Monroe.

❝ Boyer delivers big time with
a witty mystery
that is fun, radiant,
and impossible to put down! **❞**

— Darynda Jones,
New York Times Bestselling Author

NOTES

DESIGNED to death

by CHRISTINA FREEBURN

I plucked a copy of the special issue of *Making Legacies* magazine from the stack on the cropping-turned-signing table. *Introducing the New Divas* was emblazed across the front in a bold, bubblegum pink font. The heavier cardboard style cover of the issue kept the magazine firm as it rested on my palm. I ran my hand over the slick surface and hoped having an official Life Artist Diva in residence would help bring fans to our store in Eden, West Virginia.

66 Freeburn's second installment in her scrapbooking mystery series is full of small-town intrigue, twists and turns, and plenty of heart. **99**

— Mollie Cox Bryan,
Agatha Award Finalist, *Scrapbook of Secrets*

___ / ___ / ___

NOTES

_____ / _____ / _____

NOTES

KILLER IMAGE

BY WENDY TYSON

Arnie Feldman needed a drink, a bath, and a screw, in that order. But no one was home, except Sasha's dog. Stupid beast. Arnie picked up the Chihuahua, tossed him in the study and slammed the door. Then he took off his shoes, careful not to scuff the newly polished leather, and placed them next to the foyer closet. Sasha could put them away later. Where was she, anyway? And where was Ethan? He glanced at his watch: 7:18. Too late for shopping. Who was he kidding? For his wife, it was never too late to shop.

66 An intriguing psychological thriller...it's dark and hopeful at the same time. Five stars! **99**

— Lynn Farris,
Mystery Books Examiner for Examiner.com

NOTES

BURIED LEADS
by LynDee Walker

Dead people can have the worst timing.

After a ridiculously long day of deadlines, criminals, and cops who did not want to talk to me, I wanted a hot bath and my warm bed. Was that too much for a girl to ask? Apparently so, because there I was, traipsing around the woods looking for a half-eaten dead guy who got himself discovered at eleven o'clock. At night.

The glamorous life of a journalist.

66 Nichelle Clarke is back again...
Very smartly written
and cleverly plotted,
with a nifty surprise ending! 99

— Laura Levine,
Author of the Jaine Austen Mystery Series

NOTES

_____ / _____ / _____

NOTES

HiJACK in ABSTRACT

by LARISSA REINHART

There are many places you don't want to be at zero dark thirty, but I've got a personal top three. One is the ER. Second is a police station. The third is your ex-boyfriend's bedroom.

Thank God Almighty I was not in number three. Stupid does catch me occasionally, but not this night. I was nowhere near an ex-boyfriend's bedroom.

NOTES

diner IMPOSSIBLE
by Terri L. Austin

They say you never forget your first time, but of course some firsts are more memorable than others. A first kiss. A first car. That first disastrous sexual encounter with a prom date because you figured what the hell, might as well see what everyone's talking about. Turns out, they were talking about something completely different than what James Palmer and I did, fumbling around in the back of a white limo. The point is this: life's chock full of first times. Some good, some bad, but all of them are turning points, dividing lines separating your life into befores and afters.

66 Rose slips into her amateur sleuth persona and the fun begins. I urge you to tag along. I promise you'll have a grand old time. 99

— *CriminalElement.com*

NOTES

_____ / _____ / _____

NOTES

HEARTACHE MOTEL

THREE INTERCONNECTED MYSTERY NOVELLAS

DINERS KEEPERS, LOSERS WEEPERS by Terri L. Austin
Christmastime at Ma's Diner was busier than ever. Despite
the saggy gold tinsel dangling above the plate glass window
and the depressing Neil Sedaka carols Ma insisted on playing,
we had more customers than chairs.

QUICK SKETCH by Larissa Reinhart
In the setting December sun, the fluorescent Heartache sign
flickered to life and then winked into retirement. Evidently
most of the bulbs had not been replaced since the Heartache
Motel's Memphis inception, somewhere between 1962 and
1983, give or take a lost decade.

DATELINE MEMPHIS by LynDee Walker
Christmas vacation lesson number one: don't leave hotel
reservations to chance, especially when visiting a major
tourist attraction. Lesson two: crime reporters don't get
holidays. Criminals, it turns out, are everywhere.

66 It is the perfect rainy day, sunny day,
I don't feel like getting out of bed book! 99

— Heather Haven,
Author of the Alvarez Family Mysteries

_____ / _____ / _____

NOTES

DOUBLEDIP

by Gretchen Archer

The Gulf Coast has two seasons: scorching and slot tournament.

It goes from one to the other in a matter of hours.

I grew up two-hundred miles north of here in Pine Apple, Alabama, where I was a police officer for six years and where we had four seasons, the familiar ones. I moved to the Gulf to take a job with an undercover security team at the Bellissimo Resort and Casino, the tallest building in the state of Mississippi, on the beach in Biloxi, and where there are only two temperatures: 120° and 21°.

66 A smart, snappy writer who hits your funny bone! **99**

— Janet Evanovich

_____ / _____ / _____

NOTES

_____ / _____ / _____

NOTES

PIRATE VISHNU

BY GIGI PANDIAN

The first time Anand Paravar died, he was fifteen years old.

The year was 1895. Typhoid fever swept through the south of India. The sickness wended its way through the Kingdom of Travancore. It swept across its beaches of multicolored sand, through the banyan trees, and along the winding streets of the villages. The monsoon season brought uncharacteristically strong rain to the southern tip of India that year—and along with it the disease.

66 A delicious tall tale about
a treasure map, magicians,
musicians, mysterious ancestors,
and a few bad men. 99

— *Mystery Scene Magazine*

NOTES

Pillow Stalk

by Diane Vallere

"Mr. Johnson, I'm calling to discuss the disposition of your mother's estate," I said into the yellow donut phone.

"Are you a lawyer?" asked a gruff voice on the other end of a crackly line.

"No, sir, I'm an interior decorator. Madison Night. I own Mad for Mod on Greenville Avenue." I paused, giving him time to react. When he didn't, I continued. "I assure you I mean no disrespect. In my experience, you are about to be faced with the time consuming challenge of handling your mother's affairs, and I am in a position to take a portion of that challenge off your to-do list." Internally, I cringed at the holier-than-thou tone that had crept into my voice. It was an oral knee-jerk reaction to people not taking me seriously. "Mad for Mod specializes in mid-century modern design. Your mother's house was–"

66 Instead of clashing,
humor and danger meld perfectly,
and there's a cliffhanger
that will make your jaw drop! 99

— RT Book Reviews

___ / ___ / ___

NOTES

___ / ___ / ___

NOTES

CIRCLE OF INFLUENCE

BY ANNETTE DASHOFY

Zoe Chambers eased the Monongahela County EMS ambulance to a stop next to a heap of dirty snow. The overhead dusk-to-dawn light revealed a fire hydrant poking through the mound, which explained why that spot remained vacant on a street otherwise packed with cars, trucks and SUVs. No one would ticket an emergency vehicle, though. At least, no one had in the dozen years she'd been a paramedic. She hoped tonight wouldn't be a first.

66 Dashofy takes
small town politics
and long simmering feuds,
adds colorful characters, and
brings it to a boil
in a welcome new series. 99

— Hallie Ephron,
Author of *There Was an Old Woman*

NOTES

That Touch of Ink
by Diane Vallere

The money arrived on a Tuesday. Five thousand dollars, wrapped in a sheet of newsprint. It wasn't a stack of carefully counted bills. It wasn't a check. Nobody owed me money. But the fact that this sum of five thousand dollars came with the rest of the mail, in the form of one bill, made the situation all the worse. Only one person in the world would send me a five thousand dollar bill.

Brad Turlington. The man I thought I knew better than anyone I'd ever known in my life, until the day I learned he was a stranger.

66 The suspense is intense,
the plot is hot, and
the style is to die for.
A thoroughly entertaining entry
in this enjoyable series! 99

— Catriona McPherson,
Agatha Award-Winning Author

_____ / _____ / _____

NOTES

_____ / _____ / _____

NOTES

SMALL TOWN SPIN
by LynDee Walker

The news doesn't take sick days.

Generally, the number of blocks on a calendar that I don't work are rarer than comfortable shoes at a runway show. But four hours into a double shot of Claritin and DayQuil on a sunny April afternoon, I still felt like I'd been hit by a truck, and had only managed to finish one story.

"I think pollen season has won the afternoon, kiddo," my editor said, eyeballing me from the doorway of my cubicle. I tried to lift my head to reply, but dropped it back to my desk with a dull thunk.

66 A riveting mystery
with big ideas and wonderful characters...
a fantastic addition to the
Headlines in High Heels series. 99

— Duffy Brown,
Agatha Award-Winning Author

_____ / _____ / _____

NOTES

WHACK JOB

By Kendel Lynn

A guy walks into a bar with a satchel full of cash in one hand and a banana in the other. He approaches a man sitting at a corner table and asks, what will you give me for this banana? The man looks him over and says, how about this? He pulls out a gun and shoots banana guy point blank.

Unfortunately, there's no punch line. I know this because I was halfway through a corned beef on marble rye when the banana guy crashed into me. It took one second for the shooter to leap over the table, another second to grab the satchel, and two more to make it out the front door.

❝ A must-read mystery with
a sassy sleuth,
a Wonderland of quirky characters, and
a fabulous island setting
that will keep you turning pages. **❞**

— Riley Adams,
Author of the Memphis BBQ Mysteries

NOTES

the breakup doctor
by phoebe fox

It was Sasha who gave me the idea. The day my life was literally reduced to rubble by a wrecking ball, my best friend called at six a.m., while I was still lying in Kendall's king-size bed at his condo, our legs entwined and sleep crusted in our eyes.

I answered my cell groggily and heard Sasha's voice. "Can you come over?" There was a familiar hint of distress in her tone.

66 Warm, charming,
and flat-out funny—
a delightful debut! 99

— Sarah Bird,
Bestselling Author of *The Boyfriend School*

Title:

Author:

Tidbits:

Title:

Author:

Tidbits:

Title:

Author:

Tidbits:

Title:

Author:

Tidbits:

Title:

Author:

Tidbits:

Title:

Author:

Tidbits:

Title:

Author:

Tidbits:

Title:

Author:

Tidbits:

Title:

Author:

Tidbits:

Title:

Author:

Tidbits:

Title:

Author:

Tidbits:

Title:

Author:

Tidbits:

Title:

Author:

Tidbits:

Title:

Author:

Tidbits:

TBR LIST

Title:

Author:

Tidbits:

Title:

Author:

Tidbits:

Title:

Author:

Tidbits:

Title:

Author:

Tidbits:

Title: _____

Author: _____

Tidbits: _____

Title: _____

Author: _____

Tidbits: _____

Title: _____

Author: _____

Tidbits: _____

Title: _____

Author: _____

Tidbits: _____

Title: _____

Author: _____

Tidbits: _____

Title: _____

Author: _____

Tidbits: _____

Title:

Author:

Tidbits:

Title:

Author:

Tidbits:

Title:

Author:

Tidbits:

Title:

Author:

Tidbits:

Title:

Author:

Tidbits:

Title:

Author:

Tidbits:

Title:

Author:

Tidbits:

Title:

Author:

Tidbits:

Title:

Author:

Tidbits:

Title:

Author:

Tidbits:

Title:

Author:

Tidbits:

Title:

Author:

Tidbits:

Title: _____

Author: _____

Tidbits: _____

Title: _____

Author: _____

Tidbits: _____

TBR LIST

Title: _____

Author: _____

Tidbits: _____

Title: _____

Author: _____

Tidbits: _____

Title: _____

Author: _____

Tidbits: _____

Title: _____

Author: _____

Tidbits: _____

SUNDAY	MONDAY	TUESDAY	WEDNESDAY
			1 New Year's Day
5	6	7	8
12	13	14	15
19	20 Martin Luther King Jr. Day	21	22
26	27	28	29

THURSDAY	FRIDAY	SATURDAY	
2	3	4	**FEBRUARY**
9	10	11	**MARCH**
16	17	18	**APRIL**
23	24	25	**MAY**
30	31		**JUNE**

FEBRUARY

S	M	T	W	T	F	S
						1
2	3	4	5	6	7	8
9	10	11	12	13	14	15
16	17	18	19	20	21	22
23	24	25	26	27	28	

MARCH

S	M	T	W	T	F	S
						1
2	3	4	5	6	7	8
9	10	11	12	13	14	15
16	17	18	19	20	21	22
23	24	25	26	27	28	29
30	31					

APRIL

S	M	T	W	T	F	S
		1	2	3	4	5
6	7	8	9	10	11	12
13	14	15	16	17	18	19
20	21	22	23	24	25	26
27	28	29	30			

MAY

S	M	T	W	T	F	S
				1	2	3
4	5	6	7	8	9	10
11	12	13	14	15	16	17
18	19	20	21	22	23	24
25	26	27	28	29	30	31

JUNE

S	M	T	W	T	F	S
1	2	3	4	5	6	7
8	9	10	11	12	13	14
15	16	17	18	19	20	21
22	23	24	25	26	27	28
29	30					

Chinese New Year

PLANNER

SUNDAY	MONDAY	TUESDAY	WEDNESDAY
2 Groundhog Day	3	4	5
9	10	11	12
16	17 Presidents' Day	18	19
23	24	25	26

FEBRUARY 2014

THURSDAY	FRIDAY	SATURDAY	
		1 Cape Fear Crime Festival FEB 1	**MARCH** S M T W T F S 1 2 3 4 5 6 7 8 9 10 11 12 13 14 15 16 17 18 19 20 21 22 23 24 25 26 27 28 29 30 31
6	**7** Love is Murder FEB 7 - 9	**8**	**APRIL** S M T W T F S 1 2 3 4 5 6 7 8 9 10 11 12 13 14 15 16 17 18 19 20 21 22 23 24 25 26 27 28 29 30
13 Savannah Book Festival FEB 13 - 16	**14** Valentine's Day	**15**	**MAY** S M T W T F S 1 2 3 4 5 6 7 8 9 10 11 12 13 14 15 16 17 18 19 20 21 22 23 24 25 26 27 28 29 30 31
20	**21**	**22**	**JUNE** S M T W T F S 1 2 3 4 5 6 7 8 9 10 11 12 13 14 15 16 17 18 19 20 21 22 23 24 25 26 27 28 29 30
27 Sleuthfest FEB 27 - MAR 2	**28**		**JULY** S M T W T F S 1 2 3 4 5 6 7 8 9 10 11 12 13 14 15 16 17 18 19 20 21 22 23 24 25 26 27 28 29 30 31

PLANNER

SUNDAY	MONDAY	TUESDAY	WEDNESDAY
2	3	4	5 Ash Wednesday
9 Daylight Saving Time Begins	10	11	12
16	17 St. Patrick's Day	18	19 Virginia Festival of the Book MAR 19 - 23
23	24	25	26
30	31		

THURSDAY	FRIDAY	SATURDAY	
		1	**APRIL** S M T W T F S 1 2 3 4 5 6 7 8 9 10 11 12 13 14 15 16 17 18 19 20 21 22 23 24 25 26 27 28 29 30
6	**7**	**8**	**MAY** S M T W T F S 1 2 3 4 5 6 7 8 9 10 11 12 13 14 15 16 17 18 19 20 21 22 23 24 25 26 27 28 29 30 31
13	**14**	**15** Tucson Festival of Books MAR 14 - 15	**JUNE** S M T W T F S 1 2 3 4 5 6 7 8 9 10 11 12 13 14 15 16 17 18 19 20 21 22 23 24 25 26 27 28 29 30
20 First Day of Spring Left Coast Crime MAR 20 - 23	**21**	**22**	**JULY** S M T W T F S 1 2 3 4 5 6 7 8 9 10 11 12 13 14 15 16 17 18 19 20 21 22 23 24 25 26 27 28 29 30 31
27	**28**	**29**	**AUGUST** S M T W T F S 1 2 3 4 5 6 7 8 9 10 11 12 13 14 15 16 17 18 19 20 21 22 23 24 25 26 27 28 29 30 31

PLANNER

SUNDAY	MONDAY	TUESDAY	WEDNESDAY
		1 April Fool's Day	2
6	7	8 London Book Fair APR 8 - 10	9
13 Palm Sunday	14 Passover (Begins at Sundown)	15	16
20 Easter	21 Easter Monday (C)	22 Earth Day	23
27	28	29	30

THURSDAY	FRIDAY	SATURDAY	
3	4	5	**MAY**
			S M T W T F S
			1 2 3
			4 5 6 7 8 9 10
			11 12 13 14 15 16 17
			18 19 20 21 22 23 24
		San Antonio Book Festival APR 5	25 26 27 28 29 30 31
10	11	12	**JUNE**
			S M T W T F S
			1 2 3 4 5 6 7
			8 9 10 11 12 13 14
			15 16 17 18 19 20 21
			22 23 24 25 26 27 28
		LA Times Festival of Books APR 12 - 13	29 30
17	18	19	**JULY**
			S M T W T F S
			1 2 3 4 5
			6 7 8 9 10 11 12
			13 14 15 16 17 18 19
		Alabama Book Festival APR 19	20 21 22 23 24 25 26
	Good Friday		27 28 29 30 31
24	25	26	**AUGUST**
			S M T W T F S
			1 2
			3 4 5 6 7 8 9
			10 11 12 13 14 15 16
			17 18 19 20 21 22 23
Arkansas Literary Festival APR 24 - 27			24 25 26 27 28 29 30
			31

SEPTEMBER

S M T W T F S
1 2 3 4 5 6
7 8 9 10 11 12 13
14 15 16 17 18 19 20
21 22 23 24 25 26 27
28 29 30

PLANNER

SUNDAY	MONDAY	TUESDAY	WEDNESDAY
4	5	6	7 MLB Festival of Mystery MAY 7
11 Mother's Day	12	13 RT Booklovers Convention MAY 13 - 18	14
18	19 Victoria Day (C)	20	21
25	26 Memorial Day	27	28 Book Expo America MAY 28 -31

THURSDAY	FRIDAY	SATURDAY	
1	**2**	**3**	**JUNE**
			S M T W T F S
			1 2 3 4 5 6 7
			8 9 10 11 12 13 14
			15 16 17 18 19 20 21
			22 23 24 25 26 27 28
Edgar Awards Banquet MAY 1	Malice Domestic MAY 2 - 4	Agatha Awards Banquet MAY 3	29 30
8	**9**	**10**	**JULY**
			S M T W T F S
			1 2 3 4 5
			6 7 8 9 10 11 12
			13 14 15 16 17 18 19
			20 21 22 23 24 25 26
			27 28 29 30 31
15	**16**	**17**	**AUGUST**
			S M T W T F S
			1 2
			3 4 5 6 7 8 9
			10 11 12 13 14 15 16
			17 18 19 20 21 22 23
			24 25 26 27 28 29 30
CrimeFest (UK) MAY 15 - 18	South Carolina Book Festival MAY 16 - 18	Armed Forces Day	31
22	**23**	**24**	**SEPTEMBER**
			S M T W T F S
			1 2 3 4 5 6
			7 8 9 10 11 12 13
			14 15 16 17 18 19 20
			21 22 23 24 25 26 27
			28 29 30
29	**30**	**31**	**OCTOBER**
			S M T W T F S
			1 2 3 4
			5 6 7 8 9 10 11
			12 13 14 15 16 17 18
			19 20 21 22 23 24 25
			26 27 28 29 30 31

PLANNER

SUNDAY	MONDAY	TUESDAY	WEDNESDAY
1	2 Nancy Drew Sleuths Con JUN 2 - 8	3	4
8	9	10	11
15 Father's Day	16	17	18
22	23	24	25
29	30		

THURSDAY	FRIDAY	SATURDAY	
5	6	7 Printers Row Lit Fest JUN 7 - 8	**JULY** S M T W T F S 1 2 3 4 5 6 7 8 9 10 11 12 13 14 15 16 17 18 19 20 21 22 23 24 25 26 27 28 29 30 31
12	13	14 Flag Day	**AUGUST** S M T W T F S 1 2 3 4 5 6 7 8 9 10 11 12 13 14 15 16 17 18 19 20 21 22 23 24 25 26 27 28 29 30 31
19	20	21 First Day of Summer	**SEPTEMBER** S M T W T F S 1 2 3 4 5 6 7 8 9 10 11 12 13 14 15 16 17 18 19 20 21 22 23 24 25 26 27 28 29 30
26 ALA Annual Conference JUN 26 - JUL 1	27	28 Ramadan (Begins at Sundown)	**OCTOBER** S M T W T F S 1 2 3 4 5 6 7 8 9 10 11 12 13 14 15 16 17 18 19 20 21 22 23 24 25 26 27 28 29 30 31
			NOVEMBER S M T W T F S 1 2 3 4 5 6 7 8 9 10 11 12 13 14 15 16 17 18 19 20 21 22 23 24 25 26 27 28 29 30

PLANNER

SUNDAY	MONDAY	TUESDAY	WEDNESDAY
		1 Canada Day (C)	2
6	7	8 ThrillerFest JUL 8 - 12	9
13	14	15	16
20	21	22	23 RWA Annual Conference JUL 23 - 26
27	28	29	30

THURSDAY	FRIDAY	SATURDAY	
3	4	5	**AUGUST**
			S M T W T F S
			1 2
			3 4 5 6 7 8 9
			10 11 12 13 14 15 16
			17 18 19 20 21 22 23
			24 25 26 27 28 29 30
	Independence Day		31
10	11	12	**SEPTEMBER**
			S M T W T F S
			1 2 3 4 5 6
			7 8 9 10 11 12 13
			14 15 16 17 18 19 20
			21 22 23 24 25 26 27
			28 29 30
17	18	19	**OCTOBER**
			S M T W T F S
			1 2 3 4
			5 6 7 8 9 10 11
			12 13 14 15 16 17 18
			19 20 21 22 23 24 25
			26 27 28 29 30 31
24	25	26	**NOVEMBER**
			S M T W T F S
			1
			2 3 4 5 6 7 8
			9 10 11 12 13 14 15
			16 17 18 19 20 21 22
			23 24 25 26 27 28 29
			30
31			**DECEMBER**
			S M T W T F S
			1 2 3 4 5 6
			7 8 9 10 11 12 13
			14 15 16 17 18 19 20
			21 22 23 24 25 26 27
			28 29 30 31

PLANNER

SUNDAY	MONDAY	TUESDAY	WEDNESDAY
3	4 Civic Holiday (C)	5	6
10	11	12	13
17	18	19	20
24 31	25	26	27

THURSDAY	FRIDAY	SATURDAY	
	1	2	**SEPTEMBER** S M T W T F S 1 2 3 4 5 6 7 8 9 10 11 12 13 14 15 16 17 18 19 20 21 22 23 24 25 26 27 28 29 30
7	8	9	**OCTOBER** S M T W T F S 1 2 3 4 5 6 7 8 9 10 11 12 13 14 15 16 17 18 19 20 21 22 23 24 25 26 27 28 29 30 31
14	15	16	**NOVEMBER** S M T W T F S 1 2 3 4 5 6 7 8 9 10 11 12 13 14 15 16 17 18 19 20 21 22 23 24 25 26 27 28 29 30
21	22	23	**DECEMBER** S M T W T F S 1 2 3 4 5 6 7 8 9 10 11 12 13 14 15 16 17 18 19 20 21 22 23 24 25 26 27 28 29 30 31
Killer Nashville AUG 21 - 24			
28	29	30	**JANUARY** S M T W T F S 1 2 3 4 5 6 7 8 9 10 11 12 13 14 15 16 17 18 19 20 21 22 23 24 25 26 27 28 29 30 31
	Decatur Book Festival AUG 29 - 30	National Book Festival AUG 30	

PLANNER

SUNDAY	MONDAY	TUESDAY	WEDNESDAY
	1 Labor Day	2	3
7	8	9	10
14	15	16	17
21 Brooklyn Book Festival SEP 21	22 First Day of Autumn	23	24 Rosh Hashanah (Begins at Sundown)
28	29	30	

SEPTEMBER 2014

THURSDAY	FRIDAY	SATURDAY	
4	5	6	**OCTOBER** S M T W T F S 1 2 3 4 5 6 7 8 9 10 11 12 13 14 15 16 17 18 19 20 21 22 23 24 25 26 27 28 29 30 31
11	12	13	**NOVEMBER** S M T W T F S 1 2 3 4 5 6 7 8 9 10 11 12 13 14 15 16 17 18 19 20 21 22 23 24 25 26 27 28 29 30
Patriot Day			
18	19	20	**DECEMBER** S M T W T F S 1 2 3 4 5 6 7 8 9 10 11 12 13 14 15 16 17 18 19 20 21 22 23 24 25 26 27 28 29 30 31
25	26	27	**JANUARY** S M T W T F S 1 2 3 4 5 6 7 8 9 10 11 12 13 14 15 16 17 18 19 20 21 22 23 24 25 26 27 28 29 30 31
			FEBRUARY S M T W T F S 1 2 3 4 5 6 7 8 9 10 11 12 13 14 15 16 17 18 19 20 21 22 23 24 25 26 27 28

PLANNER

SUNDAY	MONDAY	TUESDAY	WEDNESDAY
			1
5	6	7	8 Frankfurt Book Fair OCT 8 - 12
12	13 Columbus Day Thanksgiving (C)	14 Virginia Literary Festival OCT 14 - 19	15
19	20	21	22
26	27	28	29

_____

_____

_____

OCTOBER 2014

THURSDAY	FRIDAY	SATURDAY	
2	3	4	**NOVEMBER** S M T W T F S 1 2 3 4 5 6 7 8 9 10 11 12 13 14 15 16 17 18 19 20 21 22 23 24 25 26 27 28 29 30
	Yom Kippur (Begins at Sundown)		
9	10	11	**DECEMBER** S M T W T F S 1 2 3 4 5 6 7 8 9 10 11 12 13 14 15 16 17 18 19 20 21 22 23 24 25 26 27 28 29 30 31
16	17	18	**JANUARY** S M T W T F S 1 2 3 4 5 6 7 8 9 10 11 12 13 14 15 16 17 18 19 20 21 22 23 24 25 26 27 28 29 30 31
Wisconsin Book Festival OCT 16 - 19			
23	24	25	**FEBRUARY** S M T W T F S 1 2 3 4 5 6 7 8 9 10 11 12 13 14 15 16 17 18 19 20 21 22 23 24 25 26 27 28
	United Nations Day	Texas Book Festival OCT 25 - 26	
30	31		**MARCH** S M T W T F S 1 2 3 4 5 6 7 8 9 10 11 12 13 14 15 16 17 18 19 20 21 22 23 24 25 26 27 28 29 30 31
	Halloween		

PLANNER

SUNDAY	MONDAY	TUESDAY	WEDNESDAY
2 Daylight Saving Time Ends	3	4 Election Day	5
9	10	11 Veterans Day Remembrance Day (C)	12
16 Miami Book Fair TBD	17	18	19
23 30	24	25	26

NOVEMBER 2014

THURSDAY	FRIDAY	SATURDAY	
		1 Louisiana Book Festival NOV 1	**DECEMBER** S M T W T F S 1 2 3 4 5 6 7 8 9 10 11 12 13 14 15 16 17 18 19 20 21 22 23 24 25 26 27 28 29 30 31
6	7 New England Crime Bake NOV 7 - 9	8	**JANUARY** S M T W T F S 1 2 3 4 5 6 7 8 9 10 11 12 13 14 15 16 17 18 19 20 21 22 23 24 25 26 27 28 29 30 31
13 Bouchercon NOV 13 - 16	14	15	**FEBRUARY** S M T W T F S 1 2 3 4 5 6 7 8 9 10 11 12 13 14 15 16 17 18 19 20 21 22 23 24 25 26 27 28
20	21	22	**MARCH** S M T W T F S 1 2 3 4 5 6 7 8 9 10 11 12 13 14 15 16 17 18 19 20 21 22 23 24 25 26 27 28 29 30 31
27 Thanksgiving	28	29	**APRIL** S M T W T F S 1 2 3 4 5 6 7 8 9 10 11 12 13 14 15 16 17 18 19 20 21 22 23 24 25 26 27 28 29 30

PLANNER

SUNDAY	MONDAY	TUESDAY	WEDNESDAY
	1	2	3
7 Pearl Harbor Day	8	9	10
14	15	16 Hanukkah (Begins at Sundown)	17
21 First Day of Winter	22	23	24
28	29	30	31 New Year's Eve

THURSDAY	FRIDAY	SATURDAY	
4	5	6	**JANUARY** S M T W T F S 1 2 3 4 5 6 7 8 9 10 11 12 13 14 15 16 17 18 19 20 21 22 23 24 25 26 27 28 29 30 31
11	12	13	**FEBRUARY** S M T W T F S 1 2 3 4 5 6 7 8 9 10 11 12 13 14 15 16 17 18 19 20 21 22 23 24 25 26 27 28
18	19	20	**MARCH** S M T W T F S 1 2 3 4 5 6 7 8 9 10 11 12 13 14 15 16 17 18 19 20 21 22 23 24 25 26 27 28 29 30 31
25 Christmas	26 Boxing Day (C) Kwanzaa Begins	27	**APRIL** S M T W T F S 1 2 3 4 5 6 7 8 9 10 11 12 13 14 15 16 17 18 19 20 21 22 23 24 25 26 27 28 29 30
			MAY S M T W T F S 1 2 3 4 5 6 7 8 9 10 11 12 13 14 15 16 17 18 19 20 21 22 23 24 25 26 27 28 29 30 31

PLANNER

2014
FIRST LOOK BOOK

For more info on
Henery Press
or any of the books in the Hen House,
pop over to our website
www.henerypress.com

or catch us on social media
facebook.com/henerypress
twitter.com/henerypress
linkedin.com/henerypress

A special thank you to
Diane Vallere, for the inspiration,
Art Molinares, for making it our own,
Kendel Flaum, for creating the whole darn thing,
and to the Hen House Authors,
for making it all worthwhile.

HENERY PRESS
NOTES & QUOTES COLLECTION

10554797R00067

Made in the USA
San Bernardino, CA
19 April 2014